Praise For So He Hurt You, Now What?

So He Hurt You Now What, the title of this book refers to the life experience of the writer, Mrs. Nicole Cleveland and what she did to turn her pain and prison into a ministry that's helping and delivering thousands of women who have or will experience some sort of pain or disruption in their lives. Many people have experienced setbacks in their lives and never fully recover, however, this isn't the case with Nicole. Nicole reveals how you can recover all by allowing God to turn your *Pain into Purpose and your Misery into Ministry.*

This book offers the reader simple, spiritual insights, making sure each insight maps back to the Word of God. In addition to the insights, she provides short but targeted prayers to encourage you, the reader. I believe this book will change the face of our society of hurting women, as they understand that it's not over after the setback!

Pastors Cliff & Vicki Coward
Agape International Ministries Worldwide

Having personally known Nicole Cleveland for several years, I can attest that she has lived the messages she openly shares in this book. These messages are shared from the core of her journey from pain to redemption. This is why I am so very honored to be able to write this endorsement for *So He Hurt You, Now What?*

So many Women are going through severe relationship challenges and quite frankly don't know how to bounce back. "Messages of Hope for a Hurting Sister" are real solutions on how to cope when a man walks out and you're left to hold the bag. As I read this phenomenal work, I thought about if only I had this years ago! Admiration of your transparency, sincerity and how you always "keep it real."

May God continue to bless you in every area of your life and your hands that provide help to so many hurting Women.

Regina Baker, Author
How To Let Go and Let God

Life Happens; some things you have no control over. In the writing of this powerful work, *So He Hurt You Now What?,* God uses Nicole mightily. Taking you from the grave back to life, the scriptures and principles are thoroughly outlined, facilitating daily healing and unveiling the beauty that lies within. As the author shares the story of how she made it, many women will be forever transformed as they find the strength to Breathe Again.

Dr. Laequinla Hunter, Author
Ministry Shall Not Destroy My Marriage

So He Hurt You, Now What? is TRULY like the subtitle says, Messages of Hope for a Hurting Sister. For this author to be transparent in saying, "I told you I was a mess, I didn't want to pray for him and there were days I cried my eyes out" allow readers to know you may go through, BUT you're going to be okay. Nicole has once again poured out from her spirit conveying hope in the midst of every situation, accompanied with a scripture and a prayer, which is priceless. This is what women need.

What an *awesome* follow-up to S*o He Cheated, Now What?* Nicole, May GOD continue to BLESS YOU Abundantly. Continue being a *willing vessel;* it is so apparent *He is using you!*

Dr. Taffy Wagner
CEO of Money Talk Matters, LLC

Where ever you find yourself in life, whatever season you are in, *So He Hurt You, Now What?* will minister to you right where you are. I've been reminded once again . . . I can make it. Thanks Nicole for a book that will definitely change the heart of women.

Paulette Harper, Elder and Best Selling Author
Completely Whole, The Sanctuary and Living Separate Lives

Reading *So He Hurt You, Now What?* is like being curled up on a comfy couch in your PJs while sharing ice cream and comfort with your BFF.

Venus Mason Theus
Christian Wife Coach

DEDICATION

This book is dedicated to my sister friends who suffer in silence;

To the ones who come to church, but are slowly dying on the inside;

To the ones who want to give up on life;

To the ones who take care of the kids and cry while cooking dinner;

To the ones who break down while in the shower so no one hears them;

To the ones who live with panic and anxiety on a daily basis;

To the ones who barely have enough in the bank for gas money;

To the ones who play the recorder over and over in their head;

To the ones who continue to blame themselves;

To the ones with low self-esteem;

To the ones who still think this is a bad dream;

Live Again—Love Again—Dream Again—BREATHE AGAIN . . .

Introduction

On this rollercoaster we call life, each one of us has been given a choice to stay on or jump off. Oftentimes, we find ourselves stuck in the seat, when all we have to do is unbuckle the seatbelt and get off the ride. The choice is ours.

Sometimes we need a friend to shake us and tell us to "wake up".

As women, we love hard but we hurt harder. When our heart has been broken it seems like no one understands. I want you to know that I get it. I was there.

When we're hurt we can stay "stuck" or in that low place, feeling sorry for ourselves and creating the bomb.com pity party for ourselves.

So He Hurt You, Now What? Messages of Hope for a Hurting Sister is my voice in your head telling you how special you are, despite who left, walked away or betrayed you.

I want you to know they DO NOT have power over you. They don't dictate who you are or what you'll be. When we don't eat, when we beg them to come back to us and when we become that "crazy" ex, we give them our POWER. We have allowed them to control us by their negative actions towards us.

Hey Girl—Take Your POWER Back!

Yes, he may have hurt you. He may even be living with another woman, but so what! That's his loss, not yours. I want you to get out of that bed, brush your teeth, dry your eyes, get dressed and LIVE AGAIN—DREAM AGAIN—BREATHE AGAIN—We need you!

My prayer is that these messages of hope inspire you and kick start you into being the woman that God created you to be—WITH or WITHOUT him!

Stay Blessed,

Nicole

HEY GIRL,

I know it seems like you have a hole in your heart right now.

All the questions that are in your mind and the feelings you have are normal. Don't let anyone tell you otherwise. Guess what? You are human and humans have feelings as well as emotions.

I'm sure you are crying a lot right now. Girl, please . . . I didn't know I had so much water in me.

I cried RIVERS !!! One for me and one for you, too . . .

Let me share some good news with you. It gets BETTER!! Yes, I said it gets better. The pain right now is so strong it feels like it's gonna overtake you and you may even feel like giving up (I was there).

Don't give up my sister; this is not the end of you and definitely not the end of your story.

God has something specific he wants you to learn from this. I know you are thinking, Really, Lord??

Yes, it hurts—Yes, it is NOT fair. But it happened, now let's deal with it.

I love you and feel your pain. You are gonna make it through.

Suggested Scripture Reading

"Not only so, but we also rejoice in our sufferings, because we know that suffering produces perseverance; perseverance, character; and character, hope. And hope does not disappoint us, because God has poured out his love into our hearts by the Holy Spirit, whom he has given us" (Romans 5:3–5).

Prayer Starter

Father—I need you to help me. What is happening in my life right now? I feel like I am not going to make it.

I need you right now, Father. I cannot do this without you walking and talking with me. Lead me and guide me so that I do what you want me to do and not me, myself. God, I am angry, confused and just numb right now. Why did this happen to me? What do you want me to learn from this? Why Me, Lord? I thought I was doing what was right. I thought you would shield us. This is so shameful, Lord. Cover me with your protection, in Jesus' name.

Hey Girl,

I won't even ask you how you are doing. I used to hate when people asked me that question when they found out about my situation . . . I would be like . . . "Uh, duh? How do you think I feel?"

I know you are still crying and that's okay. Just don't get stuck crying to the point where you can't get anything done, like I did. I told you earlier I cried a few rivers, right? I cried so much I couldn't take care of my kids. I was no good to them. They were asking to eat and I'm crying—just a mess!

I realized I had to get it together but I had to find someone I trusted to care for my kids while God worked some things in me and out of me.

Do you have someone you trust who can help you? Is there a family member, friend, co-worker or someone in the church who can relieve you? This is very important in your healing. If you are tore up, you can't be the proper mother you need to be. You either go into depression mode or snap mode and the kids don't deserve that. Get you some help, girl!

Suggested Scripture Reading

"You are my hiding place; you will protect me from trouble and surround me with songs of deliverance. I will instruct you and teach you in the way you should go; I will counsel you and watch over you" (Psalms 32:7–8).

Prayer Starter

Father, you know I am a mess and can't take care of these kids. I can't stop crying and I'm snapping all the time. I don't want to be around anyone and I don't want anybody in my business. But Lord, I understand that I need help. Lead me to someone who has your spirit and will help me with these kids while I seek you and get myself together.

Hey Girl,

Do you find yourself angry all the time? Angry about what happened; angry about the stupid reason he gave for doing it and just plain mad. Me, Me, Me! (Raises hand) Yes, girl, that was me, too. It didn't matter if everything was going right on any given day, I would find a reason to be mad, and validate my reason ('cause, of course, I had valid reason, right?). I was hurt and he hurt me. Enough said.

God had to check me and my funky attitude. I had to realize I had more to be thankful for than most. Yes, he did what he did. Yes, he was dumb (listen to me . . . a mess), but I was here and my kids were here. They were healthy and I was in my right MIND. (Thank you, JESUS!)

Although I was hurting, I had so much to be grateful about and so do you. You need big things from God right now. You don't need something small, like a bad attitude to block your blessing and all that God has for you. Trust me; He has so much for you.

Instead of focusing on all that is wrong, take a piece of paper out and write down all the wonderful things in your life that are right.

That is enough to give God praise.

Nicole

Suggested Scripture Reading

"Make sure that nobody pays back wrong for wrong, but always try to be kind to each other and to everyone else. Be joyful always; pray continually; give thanks in all circumstances, for this is God's will for you in Christ Jesus" (1 Thessalonians 5:15–18).

Prayer Starter

Dear Lord,

Help me realize that it ain't about me and my attitude. People are watching, my kids are watching and I need you to do what I can't. Remove the anger and the bitterness from me. Remove the vengeful thinking and allow me to trust you to work everything out. Remove this unfriendly and bad disposition from me, I don't want to be the mad, bitter one. Fill me with your joy and your peace . . . in Jesus' name.

HEY GIRL,

I pray your today is better than yesterday.

I wanted to write you today to talk about internalizing and blaming yourself for what he did. Let me first tell you to stop it. Do NOT blame yourself for another grown person's actions. I did this and it almost depleted my self-esteem. I concentrated on what was wrong with me and how less of a woman I was if this could happen. What was wrong with ME? That's the question I asked myself over and over again, "Why doesn't he love ME? What did I do wrong?" Please don't do this. This is self-destructive behavior and it is unhealthy. It will cause you to go crazy, one day at a time, and that is exactly what I was doing.

I had to realize he was a grown man, responsible for his own actions and choices. I don't care what you did wrong or I did wrong; it was NOT about me and it is not about YOU. It was a choice.

Just stop it!

You were created in our Father's image and that is beautiful.

Yes, we are a piece of work, but thank God that He is not done working on us.

Suggested Scripture Reading

"For you created my inmost being; you knit me together in my mother's womb. I praise you because I am fearfully and wonderfully made; your works are wonderful, I know that full well" (Psalms 139:13–14).

Prayer Starter

Dear Lord, help me realize that this is not my fault. Remove those thoughts from my mind and the words that try to torture me in the midnight hour. I know I have things to work out but I thank you that you have not given up on me. Replace negative thoughts and words from my mind and replace them with more of the word of God. Increase my self-esteem, Lord God; let me know that I am fearfully and wonderfully made, in Jesus' name . . .

Hey Girl,

I pray your today is better than yesterday.

Why are you worrying about him? You are so focused on what he's doing and what he's not doing it's making you look crazy. Whatever you focus on will consume you and eventually overtake you. I need you to worry about you and what you are doing and not doing. (In my sister girl voice)

You may be saying, "But do you see what he's doing right now?"

Yes, his actions are very selfish right now.

Yes, he may even be acting like a fool.

You have got to keep you together. You can't be looking like the crazy, hurt, angry woman. It's not a good look, Boo. You will hear me say over and over again to just pray for him. This is a game changer. When you find yourself wanting to cuss (don't get all deep on me), pray for him.

Think about the good times you had together. Not all days were bad.

You see, the world would say don't focus on the good times because that will make you want more good times with him and be sad. I say appreciate the good times; it will cause you to smile as opposed to making you angry.

Suggested Scripture Reading

"Finally, brothers, whatever is true, whatever is noble, whatever is right, whatever is pure, whatever is lovely, whatever is admirable—if anything is excellent or praise-worthy—think about such things" (Philippians 4:8).

Prayer Starter

Lord, help me focus on the good as opposed to the bad. Bring to my memory all the happy days I once had with him and, Father, I pray for his happiness and his soul. Draw him nearer to you, Lord God, even if he is not with me. Help me, Lord.

Hey Girl,

I pray your today is better than your yesterday.

In the midst of all this pain you are experiencing, I need you to do me a favor. This may be one of the hardest things you will do, but I believe it's important.

When you have healed and are in a good place with your ex, ask him what went wrong. Was it you?

This takes maturity on both ends. I don't advice you to do this until you are in a good place with the situation. You may not like it, but you need to know. If not, you will have all kinds of questions roaming through your head.

In order to move on, you must deal with the truth.

Sit down with him in a public place (go for coffee or grab some lunch).

Ask the hard questions. What happened? Did I contribute to this? What could I have done differently?

This is not about pointing fingers, blaming or even defending yourself. When you ask the questions, be prepared for the answers.

This has nothing to do with you getting back together, but everything to do with you being free and moving on.

Suggested Scripture Reading

"Then you will know the truth, and the truth will set you free" (John 8:32).

Prayer Starter

Lord, help me with this. Teach me to be mature when I sit down with him and, Father, don't allow me to be defensive. I want to better myself, Lord, and if that is taking what he says and applying it to my life, so be it.

Hey Girl,

I pray your today is better than yesterday.

Do you have to see the person who hurt you? I was so sick to my stomach when I found out about the betrayal. It would be worse when I saw him. If you have kids, there is no way you can avoid him. I will be honest; I had mixed feelings when I saw him. One moment I wanted to cause bodily injury, because I wanted him to feel what I was feeling (I told you earlier God was still working on me, right?), and then I wanted to just cry. It was so hard, so I understand those feelings you are experiencing.

What I had to do was set boundaries and guard myself. I made myself a promise that I would not cry around him (because, truthfully, that was just pumping his ego and his flesh).

As much as you may not want to, try praying for him before he arrives. When you are praying for someone else (and not for their death) it causes you to forget about you. He is also a child of God. This was not easy in the beginning. I would be so mad at God, “Surely you don’t want me to pray for this fool!”—I told you I was a mess.

I have to be honest. In the beginning it was tough, but the more I prayed for him, it seemed like God was healing my hurt. Pray! Pray! Pray!

Suggested Scripture Reading

“This is the confidence we have in approaching God: that if we ask anything according to his will, he hears us. And if we know that he hears us—whatever we ask—we know that we have what we asked of him” (1 John 5:14–15).

Prayer Starter

Dear Lord, help me forget about myself and pray for the one who hurt me. Lord, as hard as this may be right now, allow me to lose myself in you. I understand that it is not about me but all about you being glorified. Have your way in his life right now. Let your will be done and not mine. I understand that he is just as much your child as I am. Bless him, Lord.

Hey Girl,

I pray your today is better than yesterday.

Have you compared yourself with the other woman (if there is one)?

What does she have that I don't have?

Is she prettier than I am?

Does she have a bigger booty, bigger boobs?

Does she have more education, more money, light skinned with a better job or career?

You are not alone, we've all done it.

Please stop this behavior. You will drive yourself crazy doing the comparison trivia game. It's a toxic habit that is hard to break once started.

If he left you for another woman, there is nothing you can do about it (point blank).

Yes, it hurts and it may have bruised your ego. I will never tell you to suck it up and get over it. NEVER—EVER will I say that. A broken heart takes time to heal, I don't care how saved you are. To be left for another woman hurts and sometimes the pain can be unbearable. I won't take that from you. Pain is pain. Break that nasty habit of comparing and work on your healing. Heal, my sister. Heal.

Suggested Scripture Reading

"The LORD does not look at the things man looks at. Man looks at the outward appearance,but the LORD looks at the heart" (1 Samuel 16:7).

Prayer Starter

Lord, help me not compare myself to another woman. There is nothing wrong with me because you made me just the way you wanted me. If he could not see what you see, that's his loss. Help me love me and know who I am in you. Help me, Lord.

HEY GIRL,

I forgot to tell you that you'll have good days and you will have bad ones. Although it will appear that your bad ones are winning, the good ones are about to take the lead (smile).

Some days, I would have my stuff together and be on top of the world. I would say things like,

"He don't want this. . . . Oh well, that's his loss"

"I know I look good"

"I'm just gonna do me and take care of my kids"

Then I would wake up, realize I was alone and just fall apart all over again.

Take the good days, along with the bad ones and just keep pressing. Allow yourself some bad days. It's okay; we all have them. You'll be able to look back at this and laugh because of the peace God is about to give you.

Suggested Scripture Reading

"So do not throw away your confidence; it will be richly rewarded. You need to persevere so that when you have done the will of God, you will receive what he has promised" (Hebrews 10:35–36).

Prayer Starter

Dear Lord,

Today was not one of my best days. I thank you for allowing me to make it through in my right mind.

Lord, I won't lie and say this is easy; it is far from easy. This is one of the hardest things I have had to endure in my life. I take comfort in knowing you are right here with me and that you will never leave me. Heal me, Lord.

HEY GIRL,

I pray your today is better than yesterday.

I know you get sick of folks asking how you are doing, so I won't ask you. I used to hate that. I wanted to scream, "How you think I'm doing? Right now, I feel like jumping off a bridge and doing something bad to myself but do you really care how I feel?"

Some days, I didn't know how I felt; I was numb, confused, ashamed and just wanted to go somewhere and hide until this horrific nightmare ended. I knew I had to make it through. I knew I had to keep pressing. Life was going on all around me but it seemed like I wasn't present. I was there but not there. Does that make sense?

The next time someone asks you, "How you doing?" say, "I am great and you?"

You may not feel great right now, but you are going to speak that thing into existence. We are what we say!

The power of life and death is in the tongue. Speak your way out of this. Speak how you want to feel. Speak where you want to be. Speak healing over yourself.

Suggested Scripture Reading

"The tongue has the power of life and death, and those who love it will eat its fruit" (Proverbs 18:21).

Prayer Starter

Lord, I know your word says to speak those things as though they were. As much as I feel the opposite of what the word says, show me how to trust and believe that I am what I say I am. Help me believe that the words I speak will be a reality . . . in Jesus' name. Heal me, Lord.

HEY GIRL,

I pray your today is better than yesterday.

It doesn't matter what's going on around you; YOU decide if you will be happy or sad. It doesn't matter if he left you for another woman or declared he "fell out of love" with you. That is not your problem. I repeat—that is not your problem or, frankly, your business. (That's his business and his issue, but we'll talk about him later, my focus is you and your sanity right now.)

Choose to make the best out of a bad situation and keep moving forward. Forget about taking it one day at a time. Take it one hour at a time, one moment at a time. Your life depends on this. There are so many women living with regrets because of how they responded to the hurt from a man. Don't let that be you. You are more than what he says or thinks. Get up from there and live!

Suggested Scripture Reading

"Let us fix our eyes on Jesus, the author and perfecter of our faith, who for the joy set before him endured the cross, scorning its shame, and sat down at the right hand of the throne of God" (Hebrews 12:2).

Prayer Starter

Lord, please help me to try not to figure everything out. Touch my mind right now so that I can focus on you and my healing and nothing else. Help me to not focus on why he did what he did to me. Teach me that I am only responsible for my actions. Heal me, Lord.

Hey Girl,

I pray your today is better than yesterday.

Looking at everything you have to get done can be overwhelming—kids, work, bills, church, volunteering, practice etc. . . . Most times when we try to do everything we get nothing done. The huge "To Do" list can be scary so we run from it. Don't focus on all of the things you must do, just concentrate on one at a time. Just like we take it one day at a time, you must take the items on your list one task at a time.

You paid the electric, now on to the water . . .

You decided to go back to school; now you must register. Read one chapter in the book, then tomorrow read another one.

The small victories matter just as much, if not more than the big ones.

Suggested Scripture Reading

"Commit to the Lord whatever you do, and your plans will succeed" (Proverbs 16:3).

Prayer Starter

Lord I thank you for the small victories in my life. I understand that I can't do everything and you are not even expecting that of me. Teach me how to structure my day and the tasks I have to get done. You can do all things and you are in the big stuff as well as the small stuff. Teach me Lord.

Hey Girl,

I pray your today is better than yesterday.

Be careful who you share your business with. Everyone who smiles, giggles and high fives you (even in church) is not for you. They could care less about your situation and just want to be in your business. Some will even go back and give your ex information, just to keep stuff started.

I love the mothers in the church. Those seasoned mothers, full of wisdom that can sho-nuff get a prayer through, that's who I would talk to. I spent many late nights on the phone gaining wise counsel from a few wise seniors. Find a seasoned senior, full of wisdom, that you can confide in.

Nicole

Suggested Scripture Reading

"Listen to advice and accept instruction, and in the end you will be wise" (Proverbs 19:20).

Prayer Starter

Lord, lead me to someone who will allow me to be open with my feelings, someone who will not just provide me lip service, but will lead me and guide me during this transition, someone who won't judge, but instead provide love. Lead me Lord.

Hey Girl,

I pray your today is better than yesterday.

You need some money, right?

To go from a two income household to one is a drastic change. The things you used to do, you can no longer do. This was something I thought was so unfair. May I encourage you to sit down and create a budget? You know what you have coming in and you know what's going out. Most likely, you will have to be mindful in your spending because there just isn't enough.

Look at the things you can cut. You might have to turn off the cable for a while.

Eat leftovers more often and car pool to work in order to save on gas.

Get a tablet and write everything down that you spend in a week to get a better understanding of what you are spending your money on. Have a talk with your children on how they can assist you with a spending / saving project.

This may be hard for some, but you might have to apply for assistance if need be. File for child support, spousal support, whatever type of support you can get until you can get on your feet. We all need help at one point or another in our life. There is nothing to be ashamed of.

Suggested Scripture Reading

"When pride comes, then comes disgrace, but with humility comes wisdom" (Proverbs 11:2).

Prayer Starter

Lord, you know I have pride issues and I hate asking people for help. This is so shameful and embarrassing. I get so mad that I am in this situation. If he didn't do what he did, everything would be right. How could I have ended up here? This was not the plan . . . Lord, just allow me to swallow my pride and do what needs to be done in this season. I promise, when I get out of this I will give back and help someone else who may be in this same situation. Help me Lord.

Hey Girl,

I pray your today is better than yesterday.

I know it is tight right now. You may be getting support and you may not. I know you never imagined it would be like this. People keep telling you to be strong and you are doing the best you can. I get it. The bills are increasing and the funds are decreasing. Kids are growing like weeds and it seems like folks are stealing the food you bring in the house (but the kids are just eating you out of house and home, like my momma used to say).

Seven ways to make some extra money

1. Have a yard sale.
2. Start an online business.
3. Provide childcare for friends.
4. Sell some stuff on Ebay or Craigs List.
5. Pet sit (if you like pets).
6. Are you a writer? Love to write? Become a free-lancer.

7. Are you creative? Make crafts and jewelry and sell them.

During this season in your life you must be creative as far as finances. There is money out there for you.

Suggested Scripture Reading

"Go to the ant, you sluggard; consider its ways and be wise! It has no commander, no overseer or ruler, yet it stores its provisions in summer and gathers its food at harvest" (Proverbs 6:6–8).

Prayer Starter

Lord, help me tap into my creativity to make extra money. I know I have gifts and talents that I could be compensated for. Show me what they are and lead me to someone who can help guide me in this area.

Show me, Lord.

Hey Girl,

I pray your today is better than yesterday.

What are you doing for YOU?

I know, I know. You don't have the time or the money to do anything for yourself. I said the same thing. But it is very important that you keep yourself up. Get your hair done, your nails done (even if you have to do them yourself). Get creative; put some sparkly stuff on your nails; get a design. Maybe even put some color in your hair. Get a massage. Don't have the money? Learn how to barter. This is becoming the way of the world.

The important thing is you do something for you. Don't just sit in the house, eat, watch Lifetime, and cry. This is not good. This leads to depression.

Get up and do something for yourself.

Suggested Scripture Reading

"A happy heart makes the face cheerful, but heartache crushes the spirit" (Proverbs 15:13).

Prayer Starter

Lord, you know I don't have the money to pay all my bills, let alone go and buy myself something. Help me change my mindset about this. Help me understand that taking care of myself is just as important as taking care of others, if not more. Teach me how to become happy. Help me, Lord.

Hey Girl,

I pray your today is better than yesterday.

I want you to take a trip for me. See, there you go thinking you have to spend some money . . .

As little girls, we all sat around and made plans for our future. We wanted to go to Hollywood, fly to Paris, be a dancer, doctor or even a teacher. I had dreams of singing and acting my way to the big screen. I have no singing skills whatsoever, but I still believe in my dreams (smile).

Take a trip in your mind, back to the dreams of that little girl you once were.

What did you want to be when you grew up?

What do you want to be, now that you're grown up?

What are some of the dreams you never got a chance to fulfill?

Begin to reawaken those childhood dreams. It's never too late to dream.

Suggested Scripture Reading

"Where there is no revelation, the people cast off restraint; but blessed is he who keeps the law" (Proverbs 29:18).

Prayer Starter

Lord, I remember when all I did was dream. I stopped dreaming some time ago. Give me visions as well as goals. Allow me to dream again. Show me, Lord.

Hey Girl,

I pray your today is better than your yesterday.

Has anyone told you lately how beautiful you are?

If not, I just did. You are Beautiful. When God made you he didn't just make anything. He took his time. He formed you in your mother's womb. You were created in HIS image.

When you look in the mirror what do you see?

Do you look at all that's wrong, as most of us do, or do you look at what's right?

So he hurt you, so what? That does not speak to your beauty.

Make a moment and go over to the mirror (preferably a full length one).

Look at everything that is right. From your eyes, to your nose, lips and breasts (yes, I said breasts. I had to learn to appreciate my big boobies. Folks pay for what I got, and I was blessed with mine for FREE), hips, booty, legs, skin color and fingers. Look at all of you. You are BEAUTIFUL. . . .

Suggested Scripture Reading

"How beautiful you are, my darling! Oh, how beautiful! Your eyes behind your veil are doves. Your hair is like a flock of goats descending from Mount Gilead" (Song of Solomon 4:1).

Prayer Starter

Lord, allow me to fall in love with me again. Somewhere along the way I stopped thinking I was beautiful. Teach me that I am who you created me to be and you don't make any mistakes. I am beautiful. Show me, Lord.

HEY GIRL,

I pray your today is better than your yesterday.

When was the last time you paid yourself a compliment?

We always pay other people compliments.

"I love your hair, where did you get it done?"

"You're wearing those boots."

"Love that outfit on you."

You must learn to love, accept and compliment yourself. Don't wait for someone else do it and when they don't, you get mad. Like the song says, "Encourage Yourself". You better compliment yourself, too.

Try this—look in the mirror after you get dressed (or before, whatever you like) and say, "Girl, you look good. I love that (insert outfit, hair, etc.) on you."

Say "Thank you" and keep it moving.

Suggested Scripture Reading

"Do you not know that your body is a temple of the Holy Spirit, who is in you, whom you have received from God? You are not your own;" (1 Corinthians 6:19).

Prayer Starter

Lord, help me remember that it was you who made me and not myself. Help me understand that I am a temple representing you in all that I do. Help me to appreciate every piece of me. Help me, Lord.

Hey Girl,

I pray your today is better than yesterday.

What do you like best about you?

Are you a giver? Encourager? A good listener?

What are the one or two things you love best about yourself? It could be something physical, but it could also be something you are known for.

I understand what people love about you but what do YOU love about YOU? What do you think your best quality is? Too many times we get caught up in other people's opinions of us, what they think we should be doing, who they think we should marry. It is not about them; it's all about you and your opinion right now.

Think about it. Write it down. Say it out loud. It's okay, you won't be punished for liking something about you.

Suggested Scripture Reading

"For we are God's workmanship, created in Christ Jesus to do good works, which God prepared in advance for us to do" (Ephesians 2:10).

Prayer Starter

Lord, show me how to appreciate my own qualities. I must learn how to love and appreciate me. Show me that it's okay to love myself. Teach me, Lord.

Hey Girl,

I pray your today is better than your yesterday.

Have you lost yourself trying to do everything for everybody and nothing for yourself? If so, you are not by yourself. We all need to learn how to slow down. You move so fast day by day—kids, husband, work, bills, church, events, kids' activities and the list goes on and on.

In the midst of getting your kids and spouse to where they needed to be in life you forgot about YOU. It's easy to do and most of us have done it. That's okay. Now is your time. Go back and find yourself, she's not too far away.

Rediscover who you are. What were you created to do?

Nicole

Suggested Scripture Reading

" 'For I know the plans I have for you,' declares the LORD, 'plans to prosper you and not to harm you, plans to give you hope and a future' " (Jeremiah 29:11).

Prayer Starter

Lord, who am I and what was I created to do? Allow me to find my reason for living—my purpose. I know what everybody else is supposed to be doing but don't have a clue what I am supposed to be doing. Show me, Lord.

HEY GIRL,

I pray your today is better than your yesterday.

Don't let pride stand in the way of your lights being off and your rent not being paid. In the midst of all the emotional crap I was dealing with, money (or lack of) kept being an issue as well. I was so full of pride and self I refused help, initially (that changed real quick).

When I was short on money I was so ashamed to ask to borrow money or let people know about my situation. That was pride.

Don't let pride be an issue in your life. God will send people to give to you, but you must be willing to accept it when they come. God doesn't have a bank that you can make transfers out of. He uses people to bless us. I am sure you have blessed someone in the past. Now it's your turn to reap what you have sown.

It's called a blessing, not a handout. Let them bless you, baby. When you come out of this, reach back and bless someone else.

Nicole

Suggested Scripture Reading

"See, he is puffed up; his desires are not upright—but the righteous will live by his faith" (Habakkuk 2:4).

Prayer Starter

Lord, allow me to swallow my pride and accept help from others. Don't let me hinder their blessings by not accepting their generosity. Teach me to kick pride out of the window and allow your blessings to flow.

Hey Girl,

I pray your today is better than your yesterday.

Let's talk about putting some money away for a rainy day. I know you are saying, "HELLO . . . IT'S RAINING NOW."

Yes, it may be tight but it is very important that you start putting some money up. Even if it's a dollar, just put something up. Those singles add up quickly. Save your change each day. Take all the change you have and put it in a jar for 60 days. Once you do this, you'll be surprised with what you end up with. It could be enough to fill your gas tank, buy some groceries or pay a small bill.

If you have kids you can include them in this coin hunt. Make it into a game while teaching them a valuable lesson about money.

Take that change down to your nearest coinstar, pour that change in the machine, cash that ticket and BAM! You've Got Money!

Nicole

Suggested Scripture Reading

"If anyone does not provide for his relatives, and especially for his immediate family, he has denied the faith and is worse than an unbeliever" (1 Timothy 5:8).

Prayer Starter

Lord, thank you for teaching me to appreciate all things. You are humbling me in a way I have never experienced. Thank you for teaching me valuable lessons each and every day. What we take for granted on a daily basis can mean so much to someone else. Teach me, Lord.

Hey Girl,

I pray your today is better than your yesterday.

Who owes you money?

People know the situation you are in. They know they owe you money. There is nothing wrong with asking for what is owed to you. If you are uncomfortable with this, here is a script you can use.

"Hey Tina, you know the situation I'm in right now and every little bit counts when it comes to my finances. I was calling to ask about the $XX I loaned you in XXXX (be specific) girl, I could really use that money right about now. Do you have it?"

That's it. Don't be ashamed; it's your money.

Nicole

Suggested Scripture Reading

"So I say to you: Ask and it will be given to you; seek and you will find; knock and the door will be opened to you" (Luke 11:9).

Prayer Starter

Lord, let these people give me my money. Help me Lord.

Hey Girl,

I pray your today is better than your yesterday.

Do you clip coupons?

Coupons are a great way to save money and you need to stretch your dollars right about now. You can get your kids involved by clipping and sorting the coupons. I used to save hundreds of dollars with coupons, it's not just a TV show; it's the real deal.

On Sunday, grab two papers (or you can ask a friend or co-worker to save the coupons out of the Sunday paper. Most people throw the coupons in the trash and, essentially, that's throwing money in the trash).

Clip, sort and match the coupons with the sales papers. It's not about which coupon you have; it's about the coupons you have in conjunction with the same items on sale. That's how you maximize your savings.

I know it may seem tedious in the beginning, but you'll be happy you did it in the long run. The money you will be able to save to pay for other things will surprise you. We must learn to work smarter, not harder.

Suggested Scripture Reading

"But remember the LORD your God, for it is he who gives you the ability to produce wealth, and so confirms his covenant, which he swore to your forefathers, as it is today" (Deuteronomy 8:18).

Prayer Starter

Lord, teach me how to produce wealth and save what I do have in order to be more of a blessing to the Kingdom and my family. Allow me to have the patience and willingness to learn more about this money saving opportunity. Teach me, Lord.

HEY GIRL,

I pray your today is better than your yesterday.

I'm not sure if you decided to stay or walk away. Either way, you must find a way to rebuild trust. When we are betrayed by someone we love it shatters the trust we have in people.

Just because that person betrayed you, it doesn't mean everyone will.

Start rebuilding your trust again. Not all people are liars and want to hurt you. Not all people hurt other people.

Some people really want to help you heal. Don't put a wall up that no one can tear down thinking you are protecting yourself. We all have been hurt.

Place all of your trust in the Lord, not people. When you do, your eyes are on God as opposed to every wrong the individual does. People will be people. The only person you can change is yourself. God gave you chance after chance, now you must extend the same opportunity to others. Trust in the Lord.

Pray about it and learn to trust again.

Nicole

Suggested Scripture Reading

"But blessed is the man who trusts in the LORD, whose confidence is in him. He will be like a tree planted by the water that sends out its roots by the stream. It does not fear when heat comes; its leaves are always green. It has no worries in a year of drought and never fails to bear fruit" (Jeremiah 17:7–8).

Prayer Starter

Lord, help me to trust again. I don't want to go through life lacking trust for people who really care.

Help me understand that people will be people and my trust is in you because you will never fail me.

I cannot do this by myself; only you can heal the hurt and allow me to start trusting again. Help me, Lord.

Hey Girl,

I pray your today is better than your yesterday.

Did you know we have the power to choose who will be around us?

We decide who we want in our circle and who we don't. I want you to pray about those you have around you. Seek God on this.

Everybody is NOT for you and everybody does NOT like you. That seems a bit harsh but it is what it is. Some people want you to stay hurt, busted and disgusted. You know that saying, "Misery loves company"? This is true, in the church and outside of the church.

Some folks just want to know your business and some just want to keep stuff started. You don't need this right now. There are thousands of women in prison right now because they were pressured by a so called friend to "do something about their situation." Yes, church folk in jail for killing their spouse or doing something crazy because they were acting out of emotions.

Choose your friends wisely, my sister.

Nicole

Suggested Scripture Reading

Do not be misled: "Bad company corrupts good character" (1 Corinthians 15:33).

Prayer Starter:

Lord, show me who is for me and who is not for me. I don't want any counterfeits around me during this transition in my life. I don't want anyone who means me no good. Give me a spirit of discernment. Show me, Lord.

Hey Girl,

I pray your today is better than your yesterday.

Are you still asking the question "Why Me"?

I asked this question all day, every day, in the beginning. I thought I was being punished; I thought God didn't love me and other crazy thoughts would float around in my head. I must be this really bad person.

"Why Not You?" was the response I would receive when I asked (I mean yelled) this question. (Yes, honey, I had those type of knockdown, drag out sessions with the Lord.)

Just like me, you were chosen for this assignment. Doesn't feel good but he chose you because he knew you would be able to handle it. You know that saying, "God won't put more on us than we can handle."

There is something you need to learn from this—go through with Grace.

Life is full of lessons. Learn what you need to learn and keep it moving.

You may be asking, "What in the world do I need to learn?"

Seek the Lord in prayer and He will show you.

Nicole

Suggested Scripture Reading

"Consider it pure joy, my brothers, whenever you face trials of many kinds, because you know that the testing of your faith develops perseverance. Perseverance must finish its work so that you may be mature and complete, not lacking anything. If any of you lacks wisdom, he should ask God, who gives generously to all without finding fault, and it will be given to him" (James 1:2–5).

Prayer Starter

Lord, what is the lesson I need to learn in this? Show me so that I can continue to go through with a better understanding of the outcome. Humble me and teach me not to complain in this season. Show me, Lord.

Hey Girl,

I pray your today is better than your yesterday.

Do you know people are watching you? They are watching how you go through this valley in your life right now. As believers, we go through differently than the world does. The world breaks windows and burns clothes. The world cusses and fusses and has to be right all the time.

We are different. Although our hearts may be shattered and we may feel like giving up, we know that God is yet with us. We know, even when it doesn't seem like God is near, he is yet comforting us and providing us with a peace that passes all understanding.

We go through differently.

Go through with Grace so that God can get the Glory. So that He can say, "That is my child and I chose her because she could handle it and glorify me in the process."

Suggested Scripture Reading

"Dear friends, do not be surprised at the painful trial you are suffering, as though something strange were happening to you. But rejoice that you participate in the sufferings of Christ, so that you may be overjoyed when his glory is revealed" (1 Peter 4:12–13).

Prayer Starter

Lord, continue to teach me how to go through with you on my mind. Don't allow the situation to consume me but allow me to be an example of your grace and your mercy in the process. I want the world to know that I serve a great big God who can heal broken hearts. Teach me that if I serve you I will suffer as you suffered. Teach me, Lord.

Hey Girl,

I pray your today is better than your yesterday.

I know you want to be loved and wish so much that this never happened.

Please don't get desperate and start a relationship right now. You are very vulnerable. Your emotions and feelings are all out of sync right now.

You may hurt someone because you are not ready or you may get hurt because you want so much to be married and loved again. Honey, I have been there. You may have been told nobody will ever want you after your ex left or he may have told you himself.

Let me drop a bomb on you. It doesn't matter what HE said or anybody else said. . . . God is the author and creator of your life. You exist because of Him. If HE wants you to be in a relationship, you better believe He will send your mate. You won't have to find him or chase him.

Continue to heal, my sister, and develop you and your relationship with the Lord.

He wants you all to Himself right now!

Nicole

Suggested Scripture Reading

"No temptation has seized you except what is common to man. And God is faithful; he will not let you be tempted beyond what you can bear. But when you are tempted, he will also provide a way out so that you can stand up under it" (1 Corinthians 10:13).

Prayer Starter

Lord, draw me closer to you. I want to have an intimate relationship with you. When I get certain urges and want to be loved let me know that I am loved by you. I want you to be with me in the midnight hour. Love on me, Lord, so that I do not desire to be with someone else. Heal me, Lord.

Hey Girl,

I pray your today is better than your yesterday.

So you've been thinking about giving up?

This may seem a little bit harsh, but I will ask you a question.

Who do you think you are? You are no different from anyone else.

You have been chosen to go through this storm. God chose you because He believed in you. Was he wrong? I don't think so. Our God doesn't make mistakes. People love you and like God, they believe in you, even if you don't right now. A coward gives up and you are no coward.

Get up from there, stop feeling sorry for yourself and get it together.

I Believe in You!

Nicole

Suggested Scripture Reading

"He gives strength to the weary and increases the power of the weak. Even youths grow tired and weary, and young men stumble and fall; but those who hope in the LORD will renew their strength. They will soar on wings like eagles; they will run and not grow weary, they will walk and not be faint" (Isaiah 40:29–31).

Prayer Starter

Lord, I know you are with me and your word says you will never leave me. I ask you right now, in Jesus name, for strength. I need it now more than ever before. My physical body and mind tells me I can't endure one more day but I know you are sending me help in the spirit. Thank you, Lord, for providing me with supernatural strength. Help me, Lord.

Hey Girl,

I pray your today is better than your yesterday.

You may be asking the question, "Why so much pain, Lord?"

You are not the first person to have felt this pain and you won't be the last. Once the Lord heals you, it will be your duty to help someone else. I can promise you that women will flock to you because of what you had to endure. They are called to you; I would even go as far as to say they are assigned to you. You've got to share your testimony. You've got to tell them how you made it. That is why you have been chosen to endure this pain. The Lord trusts you. He knew you could handle it and He knew you would help the next one.

Get out of your own way so that the next one won't give up; so the next one will not contemplate suicide.

Get it together so you can help your sister.

Tell it, Girl!

Suggested Scripture Reading

"My mouth will tell of your righteousness, of your salvation all day long, though I know not its measure. I will come and proclaim your mighty acts, O Sovereign LORD; I will proclaim your righteousness, yours alone. Since my youth, O God, you have taught me, and to this day I declare your marvelous deeds. Even when I am old and gray, do not forsake me, O God, till I declare your power to the next generation, your might to all who are to come. Your righteousness reaches to the skies, O God, you who have done great things. Who, O God, is like you?" (Psalm 71:15–19).

Prayer Starter

Lord, take all reservations I have away from me so that I can share my story to help another sister who may be going through what I have gone through. Help me tell the story without shame. Help me understand that it's not about me but all about you. Help me, Lord.

HEY GIRL,

I pray your today is better than yesterday.

You are more than enough. I feel I need to say that over and over again to you.

Stop thinking less of yourself. We, at times, can be our worst enemy.

It's not the enemy in others that we fear; it's the enemy in ourselves.

Yes, you can help others with your story. Yes, they will listen to you.

Honey, God does not always call the qualified, He qualifies the called, the ones that He had to train through experience. Sleepless nights, buckets of tears, loneliness and shame are a few indicators of how He qualifies you.

In the process, He is teaching you how to lean, trust and depend solely on him.

It's great to have a desire to want to perfect the story and the gifts, but an eagle doesn't learn how to fly until he is thrown out of the nest. You are learning how to fly right now, my sister.

Keep flapping those wings and soar high. Women are waiting on you.

Nicole

Suggested Scripture Reading

"The LORD himself goes before you and will be with you; he will never leave you nor forsake you. Do not be afraid; do not be discouraged" (Deuteronomy 31:8).

Prayer Starter:

Lord, thank you for choosing me and teaching me. Increase my self-esteem in you. Speak through me as only you can. Use me and take any fear that I may have away. Teach me, Lord.

Hey Girl,

I pray your today is better than your yesterday.

Have you had a heart to heart with your child (children)?

They see you hurting and they can feel that hurt. Sit down with them. Tell them why Mommy is crying. Be honest with them without talking bad about their father. My children brought me so much joy in the midst of the pain I was going through. To see them laugh, joke and play ministered to me.

I had a newborn baby who totally depended on me and that was therapeutic to me. In a strange way, I loved the way she needed me. I had purpose in the midst of my pain with her.

Don't shut the kids out. Let them in. They need their mommy right now more than ever. They are hurting in their own way. You need each other. They need to comfort you and you need to comfort them.

Suggested Scripture Reading

"If anyone does not provide for his relatives, and especially for his immediate family, he has denied the faith and is worse than an unbeliever" (2 Corinthians 1:3–4).

Prayer Starter

Lord, guide my lips and the words I use to minister to my children. Take away any bitterness and anger about their father from me so that I don't transfer it to them. Allow them to be comforted in you. Help my children heal, Lord.

Hey Girl,

I pray your today is better than your yesterday.

If you have children, make sure you tell them none of this is their fault.

Kids are so very sensitive (even those tougher-than-nails teenagers).

Just like you are playing that tape over and over in your head, so are they. Trust me; they have already thought about what they did and did not do that could have caused the break-up.

Were you arguing over the kids? Did they hear you? If so, they may think it's their fault. Make sure they know it has nothing to do with them. It's something between Mommy & Daddy and that the two of you love them very much.

My, then, 6-year-old would cry because her Daddy left and there was nothing I could do but console her and pray (it broke my heart daily). My teen started to rebel. Kids act out in very different ways. Make sure you give them extra love as they really don't understand what's going on. All they know is that they had two parents in the home and now they have just one.

Suggested Scripture Reading

"He heals the brokenhearted and binds up their wounds. He determines the number of the stars and calls them each by name. Great is our Lord and mighty in power; his understanding has no limit" (Psalms 147: 3–5).

"God is our refuge and strength, an ever-present help in trouble" (Psalms 46:1).

"For he has not despised or disdained the suffering of the afflicted one; he has not hidden his face from him but has listened to his cry for help" (Psalms 22:24).

Prayer Starter

Lord, heal my children in ways that I don't know anything about. They are hurt and confused. Draw them closer to you. Comfort them and guide them into your perfect peace. Heal my children, Lord.

Hey Girl,

I pray your today is better than your yesterday.

If you have children that are age appropriate for sports or other arts activities, sign them up. This will occupy their time and energy. This is not just good for them; it's also good for you. If they are used to Daddy coming home every day at 6pm and now 6pm comes and goes and no Daddy, they won't be sad.

This helps you because you don't have to answer those questions of where Daddy is at and watch your child's heart break over and over again.

Find some constructive activities for the kids they will enjoy in the church and outside of the church.

Some things will have a registration fee but I want you to believe in God for that being taken care of as well.

When we pray, God answers and He knows what we stand in need of.

Suggested Scripture Reading

"So do not worry, saying, 'What shall we eat?' or 'What shall we drink?' or 'What shall we wear?' For the pagans run after all these things, and your heavenly Father knows that you need them. But seek first his kingdom and his righteousness, and all these things will be given to you as well" (Matthew 6:31–33).

Prayer Starter

Lord, help me keep my children active. Let me not worry about the money we do not have, but believe that you will make a way. Allow me to have a way to pay for the extra activities. Help me, Lord.

HEY GIRL,

I pray your today is better than your yesterday.

Have you thought about your next chapter in this book called Life?

Forget about the one who hurt you, I'm not talking about him, I'm concerned about you. What do you do now? Starting today, I want you to start planning for what's next.

There are no limits to what you can do with God on your side.

Are you living your dreams?

Have you moved forward with some of the goals you had in the beginning?

Did you start then stop, putting everybody and everything in front of your dreams?

If so, you are not by yourself. Most of us do this.

Go purchase yourself a *Dream & Action Book* (a fancy title for a notebook). . . . It's not enough to just dream, you must put some work in.

Dream again!

Nicole

Suggested Scripture Reading

"Then the LORD replied: 'Write down the revelation and make it plain on tablets so that a herald may run with it. For the revelation awaits an appointed time; it speaks of the end and will not prove false. Though it linger, wait for it; it will certainly come and will not delay' " (Habakkuk 2:2–3).

Prayer Starter

Lord, teach me how to move forward with the next chapter in this book called Life. I have so many dreams that I thought were not possible until now. Show me how I can actually make my dreams become a reality. Show me, Lord.

HEY GIRL,

I Pray your today is better than your yesterday.

Why do you second guess God?

You want to trust that He's going to work it out but there is doubt lingering in the back of your mind.

You know what the word of God says about your situation but you hesitate in giving it totally to Him. Girl, don't do what I did. I would pray, go to the altar and give Him a certain situation. I would rejoice at the altar, cry and even shout, "It's gone, thank you, Jesus." As I walked back to my seat, I would drag that issue back with me as opposed to leaving it with God. This is a learned behavior. It's easy to try to take matters into our own hands. The hard part is to give it to Him and wait for the prayer to come to pass. Whatever your prayer is, give it to God and have full confidence that He will fix it.

Suggested Scripture Reading

"And without faith it is impossible to please God, because anyone who comes to him must believe that he exists and that he rewards those who earnestly seek him" (Hebrews 11:6).

Prayer Starter

Lord, I've tried on numerous occasions to fix my own life and failed miserably each time. I want to give it totally to you and not take it back. Lord, increase my faith in you. Help me, Lord.

HEY GIRL,

I pray your today is better than your yesterday.

Waiting on the Lord can be frustrating.

I know some folks will get deep on you and say they enjoy waiting on the Lord. That's not me. I'm not sure who looks forward to sitting in the holding tank. I call it the holding tank because that's where you wait for a decision. You can't move ahead of Him. You must wait. There are consequences to be made if you move too soon.

There is so much pain in the weight of the wait. It's extremely heavy and seems like the problem sits right on your heart. So what does one do? The answer to this is simple but it seems very hard.

Wait on the Lord!

In the midst of the frustration, you have got to wait. Your life depends on it.

Suggested Scripture Reading

"I waited patiently for the LORD; he turned to me and heard my cry. He lifted me out of the slimy pit, out of the mud and mire; he set my feet on a rock and gave me a firm place to stand." (Psalm 40:1–2).

Prayer Starter

Lord, teach me how to wait. Waiting is so very hard for me and I need your help. Teach me not to go ahead of you and just wait with patience and grace. Lord, teach me not to try and fix things that I can't fix. Teach me, Lord.

Hey Girl,

I pray your today is better than your yesterday.

I know you see all these couples out here that appear to have it going on.

You just knew your relationship would last the test of time in comparison to some of the couples you see and know what they are dealing with. “How could this happen to me?” has played over and over in your head.

Girlfriend—may I encourage you to not compare your situation to others? Every situation and relationship is different. If you continue to focus on others and compare theirs to yours, you will never move forward. You have no idea what really goes on behind closed doors.

Focus on you.

Suggested Scripture Reading

"For where you have envy and selfish ambition, there you find disorder and every evil practice. But the wisdom that comes from heaven is first of all pure; then peace-loving, considerate, submissive, full of mercy and good fruit, impartial and sincere" (James 3:16–17).

Prayer Starter

Lord, allow me to focus on me and my healing. I cannot afford to compare my situations with others. I pray for those couples in Jesus' name. Take envy and jealousy away from me. Heal me, Lord.

HEY GIRL,

I pray your today is better than your yesterday.

If I could run to you and give you a great big hug I would do just that. Inside you are still trying to figure out what is going on. "How could God allow this to happen?" is the question that plays over and over in your mind. You may not be perfect but God knows you tried. You didn't deserve this type of betrayal.

I will tell you again, no, it's not fair but it is life. Do you stay on the tennis court or do you jump off and get yourself together? If you don't make a decision the enemy will play tennis in your head. You will be like that ball, going back and forth across that table until you put a stop to it.

Earlier, I told you that you would have good days and then you would have bad days. You have the power to turn the bad days into good ones. It's all up to you.

Get in a quiet place and just listen to what God is trying to say to you.

Nicole

Suggested Scripture Reading

"So then, just as you received Christ Jesus as Lord, continue to live in him, rooted and built up in him, strengthened in the faith as you were taught, and overflowing with thankfulness" (Colossians 2:6–7).

Prayer Starter

Lord, I don't want to continue to go back and forth, over and over again. I need you to settle me. I give up my will for your will, Lord. Have your way in my life. Teach me how to turn bad days into good days. The power is within.

HEY GIRL,

I pray your today is better than your yesterday.

I want you to know this.

You are Strong. You are Smart. You are Successful.

When we are in our low place, the enemy wants us to believe that we are stupid, we are weak and we are pitiful. He will play tricks in our mind, if we allow him to. If we are not careful we'll start believing the lies he is planting in our minds.

Soon we will find ourselves secluded from everyone in a spirit of depression, not talking to anyone but ourselves. My sister, please don't fall for this. Get yourself up from there and be who God has called you to be. It doesn't matter what it looks like right now; God is changing things right now on your behalf. He has heard your cry and is answering your prayer.

You are strong. You are smart and you are successful.

Suggested Scripture Reading

"Now it is God who makes both us and you stand firm in Christ. He anointed us, set his seal of ownership on us, and put his Spirit in our hearts as a deposit, guaranteeing what is to come" (2 Corinthians 1:21–22).

Prayer Starter

Lord, help me know my worth. Remove all the negative thoughts from my mind. I am more and can do more because I belong to you. Heal me, Lord.

Hey Girl,

I pray your today is better than your yesterday.

Let me ask you a question.

Do you know whose you are? We are quick to jump, shout and run around the church, confessing, "I Belong to God." It feels good at the time.

When we get knocked down (which we all do) we forget who we really belong to. We were created in God's image, so God knows every aspect of who we are and what we are going through. Trust me, He knows and He cares.

We get so focused on what is going wrong in our lives that we overlook who we belong to and how He will rescue us. God is our father. He is our daddy. It doesn't matter how old we are. We will always be his little girls.

A real daddy always takes care of his little girls.

Remember who your daddy is and tell him all about it.

Suggested Scripture Reading

"How great is the love the Father has lavished on us, that we should be called children of God!" (1 John 3:1).

Prayer Starter

Lord, I'm so glad I'm your little girl. I am so honored you chose me to be in your family. There is nothing I can bring to you that will make you love me less. . . . Increase the areas in me that are lacking. I need you, Lord.

Hey Girl,

I pray your today is better than your yesterday.

I tell people all the time that God is the only thing consistent in my life. When people walk away, God is right there. When people use and abuse us, God is right there. When we are not consistent, God is right there.

That's a big one right there. When we are not consistent in our own lives, God is.

He gives us time to get ourselves together and get back on track. That's why I love Him like I do. When we are on one day and off the next, He doesn't take days off. He is always on the job.

The word of God says that He will never leave us, nor forsake us. He is an ever present help in the time of trouble and despair. When we don't know what to do, He knows.

Right now, God is the only one who can help and heal you. He was the only one who could take my mess and turn it into a message. He can do that for you, too.

Let him do it.

Nicole

Suggested Scripture Reading

"May the God of hope fill you with all joy and peace as you trust in him, so that you may overflow with hope by the power of the Holy Spirit" (Romans 15:13).

Prayer Starter

Lord, thank you for being consistent in my life. Thank you for never giving up on me. Teach me how to be consistent in my own life. Teach me, Lord.

Hey Girl,

I pray your today is better than yesterday.

It feels good to be loved, right? It's a beautiful thing when you are loved and doted on. We all want to be loved, respected and highly esteemed by our spouse or significant other.

"I just want him to love me."

But what if he doesn't love himself?

How can you expect love from someone who doesn't love himself? You can't. In order to show love to another we must first love ourselves. I see this all the time. The other person is broken. It has nothing to do with you; it's all within himself.

Love on God and He will love on you. Pray for the broken one. Pray that God will heal them, inside and out.

God is love and so are you. The word of God tells us to pray for those who use us. If you are a child of God you must know that Love covers a multitude of faults and forgiveness is key.

Put your feelings aside and pray for the one who hurt you. Do it from your heart and watch how God will heal you inside and out. The anger will turn into compassion. I don't just write this, I know this to be true because it happened in my life. It's not about what happens to us; it's all about our response. How are you responding? What are you saying to the situation? Sometimes we hinder our own healing because of our attitude while going through it. We miss the mark in the midst of our bitterness and vengeance.

The word of God says vengeance is mine saith the Lord. It is not your job to make people pay for their actions.

Go through in love and forgive everyone who hurt you.

It's not about them; it's about you and the God you serve. You can't say you serve a mighty God who has forgiven you if you are not willing to forgive someone else. The reason I can forgive much is because I have been forgiven for much. When I was wrapped up, tied up and tangled all up in sin, God saw fit to snatch me out and forgive me.

So the same forgiveness that was extended to you must be extended to those who hurt you.

We don't get to choose who will be forgiven.

Suggested Scripture Reading

"Be kind and compassionate to one another, forgiving each other, just as in Christ God forgave you" (Ephesians 4:32).

"For if you forgive men when they sin against you, your heavenly Father will also forgive you. But if you do not forgive men their sins, your Father will not forgive your sins" (Matthew 6:14–15).

Prayer Starter

Lord, help me forgive the person who hurt me. Help me understand that, in order for me to walk in total freedom, I must forgive. Just as you have forgiven me for much I must forgive everyone who has hurt me. There is nothing I can do that you will not forgive me for. And that goes the same for those who hurt me. Help me, Lord.

HEY GIRL,

I pray your today is better than your yesterday.

Every day should be better than the day before. How you start your day plays a huge role in how the day will turn out. How do you start and end your day?

Do you start with prayer or meditation in the morning? If not, I encourage you to rise 15-30 minutes earlier than usual. It may be rough in the beginning but the more you do it, the more it will become habit.

Make a pot of coffee or cup of tea and start reading the book of Psalms. Psalms is a great book to begin with because it's encouraging. The songs and poems are sure to uplift your spirit and get your day off to a great start.

Research shows that it takes 21 days to develop a habit. Start reading a few verses, then work your way up to reading a chapter or two a day. Grab a highlighter, take notes. Don't just read; digest everything you read. Make sure you understand it. If you don't fully comprehend, ask a question on Facebook or to someone you trust.

The word of God has changed my life and I know it will change yours, too.

In the evening when you lay down, end with thanksgiving. God allowed you to make it through another day.

Suggested Scripture

"But seek first his kingdom and his righteousness, and all these things will be given to you as well" (Matthew 6:33).

Prayer Starter

Lord, help me to rise early and join in fellowship with you. I want to learn more about you and your ways concerning my life. I understand that everything I need is in the word of God. Take all laziness away and give me a desire to want to know you for who you are.

Hey Girl,

I pray your today is better than yesterday.

Are you still with the one that hurt you? Have you fallen out of love with him because of the hurt?

Do you look at him with disgust and hate in your eyes? If so, you must change that and change it quickly. If you made a decision to stay and work things out, please do just that. Staying with the one that hurt you takes a great amount of love and faith. You must ask yourself. Do I look past my hurt, forgive and allow God to heal or do I let go and move on?

Take some time and answer that question. Seek the Lord. Don't answer that question with your emotions.

Say, "Lord, what would you have me do."

Suggested Scripture

"I seek you with all my heart; do not let me stray from your commands" (Psalms 119:10).

Prayer Starter

Lord, allow me to open my ears that I may hear you in the spirit. Don't allow my emotions to rule me. Show me what you would have me do with this situation. I don't want to go to the left nor the right with your approval. Guide me Lord.

HEY GIRL,

What do you see when you look in the mirror?

Do you see a fine, smart, successful woman living her life like it's golden?

- Or -

Do you see someone who is tore up, tore down and defeated?

Next time you look in the mirror, look at what's right as opposed to what's in your teeth or that strand of hair being out of place. What do you love about YOU? What do you see? What do you love that is not visible? Every day we pay compliments to others. We tell them what we love about them. Take some time and do the same for you. Try making a list of 12 things you love about yourself.

In order to attract love, you must first love yourself.

What is great about you?

What do you do well?

What do other people love about you?

What have you accomplished? I bet you there are some great attributes about you that even you forgot about. Think about them and write them down.

Things I Love About Me!

1. ______________________________

2. ______________________________

3. ______________________________

4. ______________________________

5. ______________________________

6. ______________________________

7. ______________________________

8. ______________________________

9. ______________________________

10. ______________________________

Share one or two of those things with your Facebook friends, on Twitter or with a few of your email buddies.

Example Post or Tweet—**One thing I love about myself: #iloveme #sohehurtyou**

Use these hashtags #hurtingsister #iloveme #hehurtyou #sohehurtyou

FINAL MESSAGE

HEY GIRL,

This may sound crazy but I'll just say it.

In the midst of the hurt and all the pain you are going through right now, it is imperative that you step away from your pain and help others.

You may be saying, "She must be crazy, I'm not healed nor where I need to be." You see, that's the problem. We feel like we have to be perfect and have it all together in order to help someone else. That's not the case.

When I stopped focusing on me and started to help others who were hurting, God began to heal me. My healing was tied up in helping others heal.

When you do this, you realize you are not alone. You are not crazy and you are not defeated. There are thousands, if not millions, who are where you are right now. They need to know they are not alone. They will make it and so will you. I know this, not because I read it, but because I lived it and am still living it.

The pain does not completely go away at first, but it does get easier. The excruciating pain in the middle of your chest will turn to a dull ache, then a pain that you will no longer feel. When God heals, He heals. Just as HE wipes away our sins, HE does the same thing with our pain. You'll see.

My pain comes back every now and then when I minister to hurting women. When they tell me their stories, it's like I am being healed all over again because I can literally feel what they feel and cry the same tears they are crying.

I understand that my life is not about me and neither is yours. God has trusted you with this in order to help revive those who have given up. You can be his mouthpiece. Tell your story and help somebody else. Your healing is tied up in helping the next one.

Take a chance on God and cast all your cares on him—your doubts, your fears and things you really don't want to release. Don't allow the enemy to keep you in bondage for one more second. Know your value and your worth.

You are more than a conqueror. I love you and believe in you.

Connect with me. Update me on your progress. Email me at nicoleconline@gmail.com

I am excited about your future.

Stay Blessed, my Sister!

Nicole

12 Tips to Make Your Today Better Than Yesterday

Throughout this book of messages of hope for my hurting sister, I began by saying, "I pray your today is better than yesterday."

I understand that, during a transition, you will have good days as well as bad days. The bad ones seem to get a running start but don't count the good days out, it just takes a minute for them to gain some type of speed, catch up and eventually win the race.

On the next pages you will find 12 tips to help make your today better than your yesterday.

#1 Start with a "Thank You"

Before your feet hit the ground, make sure you tell the Lord, "Thank You." It is God who woke you up to see another day, for that you must be thankful. You may not have everything you want right now, but you are in your right mind and you are here.

Start every day with thanksgiving and you are sure to make your today better than yesterday.

2 Read Something Motivational

Sometime throughout the day, make sure to make room for the word of God or whatever inspirational reading you prefer. With all the bad news we hear throughout the day you need to deposit some form of hope in your spirit.

When you read some type of motivation, you are sure to make your today better than yesterday.

#3 Create a "Get It Done" List & Get It Done

There is something about looking at a long "To Do" list compared to a "Get It Done" list. Try creating a condensed "Get It Done" list and put time limits on each task. The "To Do" list can be intimidating and overwhelming. The 'Get It Done By..." list may seem more attainable.

When you create a "Get It Done By . . ." list and actually get it done you are sure to make your today better than yesterday.

#4 What Did NOT work yesterday?

When you know better you should do better. Did something happen yesterday that got under your skin? Did it set you back and make you repent? Was it a person? If you are having a repeated problem with an individual and they keep getting on your nerves, it's not them, it's you. Stop allowing them to have control over you. Stay away from them if you can or just decide that you will not allow their actions to change your attitude. It's up to you.

When you know what sets you off and don't allow it to affect you any longer, you are sure to make your today better than yesterday.

#5 Start a Journal

Writing is therapeutic. Taking your thoughts and adding them to paper or computer can be a form of healing. How your life is going and how you want it to go is a great beginning. Document your life for the future. Some people journal for their kids and some journal to leave a legacy for the generations they will never know.

When you journal you learn new things about yourself. Journaling those unspeakable words is sure to make your today better than yesterday.

#6 Eat What You Want

Grab some comfort food and enjoy it. Don't beat yourself up, just eat it up. Don't do this every day, but I do want you to do it from time to time. Eat something you like and enjoy it. Disclaimer: Do Not Share. This is just for YOU.

When you eat something you enjoy just because you want to, you are sure to make your today better than yesterday.

#7 Me Time

Take at least 15 minutes for yourself after work each day. You've been in work mode all day and now you need to get in family/kid mode. Sometimes this is not an easy adjustment. Don't go straight to the kitchen and start preparing dinner. Take some time for you. Allow your mind to make the adjustment. Just Breathe.

When you allow yourself a few minutes to adjust from work mode to family mode, you are sure to make your today better than your yesterday.

#8 Encourage Someone

Make it a point to encourage someone each day. When we can step out of our situation and be a ray of hope for someone else it pleases God. Life is not always about us; actually, it is not really about us anyway. It's about glorifying God in what we do, how we act and react to others.

When you can encourage someone in the midst of your storm, you are sure to make your today better than yesterday.

#9 LOL

Laugh Out Loud and do it often

Laughter is medicine unto our soul. The word of God says it is medicine. Get into a habit of laughing at yourself and by yourself. You don't need a friend to laugh. Laugh at yourself. Laugh at your situation because God really has got to have a sense of humor for all that you are going through. If you are like me, you might have to laugh to keep from crying. Laugh out loud, my sister.

When you can learn to laugh at your situation and at yourself, you are sure to make your today better than yesterday.

#10 Just Dance

You don't have to be a great dancer to dance. It feels good to dance; it feels good to move. People with no type of rhythm will out dance a person who claims to have some, all because they are enjoying the dance. If you ever watch people who love to dance but, in our eyes, really can't dance, you can't help but smile because they are doing what they like to do and could care less what anyone else thinks. Try it. Turn on some music, get up and start jamming.

When you dance to the beat of your own drum and enjoy it, you are sure to make your today better than yesterday.

#11 Go to Bed Early

When was the last time you got a full 8 hours of sleep? When was the last time you took a nap during the day? Try going to bed an hour early tonight. Turn the TV off. Turn the phone off. Turn the iPad off. Make sure there are no distractions and just do it. It can wait until tomorrow. Go to Bed.

When you go to bed early and get a full night's sleep, you are sure to make your today (and your tomorrow) better than yesterday.

#12 Forgive

Forgive those who hurt you yesterday. Maybe they knew they hurt you and maybe they didn't. Either way, get it off you and forgive them. If you have to do this each and every day (with the same person) do it. It's not about them; it's all about you. It's about where you are going and what God has for you. As long as you live there will be people who will offend you and hurt you. Your responsibility is to forgive them.

Daily forgiveness ensures your today is better than your yesterday.

ENCOURAGING SCRIPTURES

"For the Spirit God gave us does not make us timid, but gives us power, love and self-discipline" (2 Timothy 1:7).

"Instead of your shame you will receive a double portion" (Isaiah 61:7a).

"I can do all this through him who gives me strength" (Philipians 4:13).

"I will say of the LORD, He is my refuge and my fortress, my God, in whom I trust" (Psalms 91:2).

" 'For I know the plans I have for you,' declairs the LORD, plans to prosper you and not to harm you, plans to give you hope and a future" (Jeremiah 29:11).

"God is our refuge and strength, an ever-present help in

trouble" (Psalms 46:1).

"I have told you these things, so that in me you may have peace. In this world you will have trouble. But take heart! I have overcome the world" (John 16:33).

"But he knows the way that I take: when he has tested me, I came forth as gold" (Job 23:10).

"And we know that all things God works for the good of those who love him, who have been called according to his purpose" (Romans 8:28).

"Even though I walk through the darkest valley, I will fear no evil, for you are with me; your rod and your staff, they comfort me" (Psalms 23:4).

"But those who hope in the LORD will renew their strength. they will soar on wings like eagles; they will run and not grow weary, they will walk and not be faint" (Isaiah 40:31).

"Trust in the LORD with all your heart and lean not on your own understanding" (Proverbs 3:5).

NOTES

About the Author

Nicole Cleveland is the founder of Breathe Again Ministries, *Breathe Again Magazine* and host of *Breathe Again Radio & TV Show.*

She has helped thousands of women extract purpose from the pain they've endured. She has a heart for those on the verge of giving up, like she once was. Her ministry and personal mission is to ensure people are not suffering in silence.

In 2010 she released her debut book, *So He Cheated, Now What?* her personal testimony of overcoming an affair in her marriage; an affair that produced a child.

God is the steady rock that stays consistent in her life. Without God, nothing she does would be possible.

Nicole is also a fundraising /retention consultant.

To book Nicole for speaking engagements or to arrange an interview, email nicole@nicoleconline.com.

Visit her online at www.nicoleconline.com

Other Works by Nicole Cleveland

Special Report: 10 Steps to Finding Me Time

So He Cheated, Now What?